Anne Trout

The long journey to the empowerment of women

2018

A widespread misconception of the historical development of humankind maintains that history is the cumulative outcome of decisions taken by men: decisions, political, military and economic, always far reaching in their consequences and always far from the influence of women. The misconception assigns a secondary, or at best the inspiring role, to women, because supposedly "behind every great man there is always a great woman".

These pages attempt at providing an explanation of how such a gross misunderstanding came to be, for the history of mankind is actually the history of the will of women.

I am aware that it is very unlikely that my message would prevail in a world ruled by women.

Similarly, I would fail if my intention was to convince you — against the traditional conception of monotheistic religions — that the good God is ruling over us while the Devil has been banished to hell. It is the good man who is condemned to hell, while the bad man, concealed under his farcical kindness, rules mankind from above with ease.

The majority of men are convinced that they enjoy a higher status than women and in consequence they subscribe to the claim that social equality for women has a basis in fact.

In order to argue against this completely unfortunate picture of historical development, firstly we need to make a short incursion into biology, just long enough to set a starting point for the explanation I will further develop.

The first thing we need to understand is a logical and inescapable simple aspect of reproduction: if a species does not reproduce, it disappears. As a consequence, all mechanisms that favour reproduction will tend to survive, and all those that don't, will not.

Homo sapiens, from the beginning of its independent journey distinct from other species of anthropoid monkeys —three to five million years ago — developed as its central survival strategy, social reproductive mechanisms based on group cooperation to achieve success. No other mammals developed the social reproductive strategy to the same extent.

The key to the success of these strategies of social reproduction is their capacity to foster altruistic behaviours where a member of the group acts to the benefit of the rest by protecting the weak until the weak become sufficiently strong to look after the next generation, and so on.

Why did the human species choose this path? The simple answer is that it worked. The development of altruistic behaviour has a positive reproductive impact, and has consequently fed the rest of the system.

To understand the impact of this factor in the whole process we need to clarify that altruism is not a behaviour invented by the human species, but is one that appears early in the development of all "social" species as a key factor. The difference with regards to the human species is that in us, given the markedly immature nature of our young, where many years are needed for them to reach maturity, altruism becomes the basis for the whole social structure.

Once we arrive at this conclusion we need to ask who is in control of the reproduction of altruism, the strong or the weak? The answer seems evident in light of the development of "altruism" in history: there is no inherent desire for the strong to serve the weak, it is simply the only outcome because acting differently would lead to the disappearance of the species, a higher calling that can only result in this type of behaviour. To express it crudely but clearly, a newborn is just a tender piece of meat for parents who have to satisfy the food needs. Why don't they eat it? They don't eat it because there are selective patterns of altruistic behaviour acting on them. Mechanisms that stem from the simple fact that if they did, our species would have disappeared long ago.

Using the above example, let us introduce a crucial notion which will allow us to understand the development of the human species: that altruistic behaviour is not a "natural" behaviour but an acquired one. Furthermore, this behaviour should be considered "antinatural" insofar that the survival of each individual depends on the immediate satisfaction of their biological needs, like nourishment and sex, while the survival of the social species depends on our capacity to deny those same needs.

In a strictly hypothetical "natural" sense, that is, leaving aside the cultural traits of our species, a newborn baby is to its father just a tasty morsel —unable to view it as the product of a sexual interaction far in the past, and appearing no more like himself than might a small monkey. But, in the same hypothetical "natural" setting, the circumstances are completely different from the point of view of the mother.

Remember that the newborn has been a part of her body for the previous nine months and that just after the birth the baby was still attached to her body by the umbilical cord. Furthermore, the baby's attempts at suckling stimulate the production of milk in her breasts as well as other various reactions, including those of a psychological kind. All of these form "naturally" strong bonds between the mother and her offspring.

Considering these circumstances, the mother will "naturally" assume the role of protector. As in other species, her first concern with regards to protecting the baby will be to control the behaviour of the potentially dangerous males around her.

But how can the mother control her surroundings effectively when she is already physically weaker than the male and now even weaker because of the efforts childbirth? The control of male behaviour, in order to be effective in terms of adaptation, must have been established somewhat earlier than the birth of children.

How then did they possibly manage to establish such behavioural control that could turn the potentially predatory male into a meek attendant, ready to take on the protection of the mother and the offspring?

The answer is fairly obvious, though it is true that nature is seldom explicit. Control is achieved through the development of strategies that cloak the real state of affairs and, at the same time, lead men to believe that they are the ones — contrary to what would be "natural" behaviour — who are really setting the rules of social behaviour.

Evidence of that, is that in any culture, the baby's first intentional utterances — such as ba-ba, pa-pa or ta-ta — are immediately interpreted by the mother to mean "papa", as she anxiously awaits the presence of the father to show him what wonderful progress the child has made.

We should ask ourselves why would a baby make such a useless effort? It spends the whole day with its mother, whom we can imagine the baby adores. It is always making its greatest efforts to improve its communication with its mother, but strangely enough, its first conscious sounds result in summoning a person it rarely sees during the day.

The desperate child subject to this stress soon learns that he is using the wrong sound, because every time he calls his mother, this strange being turns up, therefore he must change so he can summon his beloved mother: "ma ma".

This symbolises the beginning of the ascendency of the female: to deconstruct the facts so they appear as an achievement of the male. It is also the end of the natural history of the species, since the need to assure reproduction has been now clearly established: that is, males who are sufficiently aggressive towards the outside of the home in order to protect it — including the procurement of food — and sufficiently gentle towards the interior, in order to knit strong bonds with his offspring and their mother.

This subtle but supremely strong web has been knitted for three million years, ever since *Homo sapiens* took a different evolutionary path from that of its cousins, the anthropomorphic monkeys. This most original path, essentially a mechanism of adaptation to the environment, consisted of practices "cultural" in nature. These human-created behaviours stem from our own potential, as opposed to those that have an instinctive- or genetically-determined nature.

In order to understand how this process works, we need to abandon our inclination to think of ourselves as individuals, with a unique and personal existence separate from that of others, and that we are in command, generally speaking, of our actions.

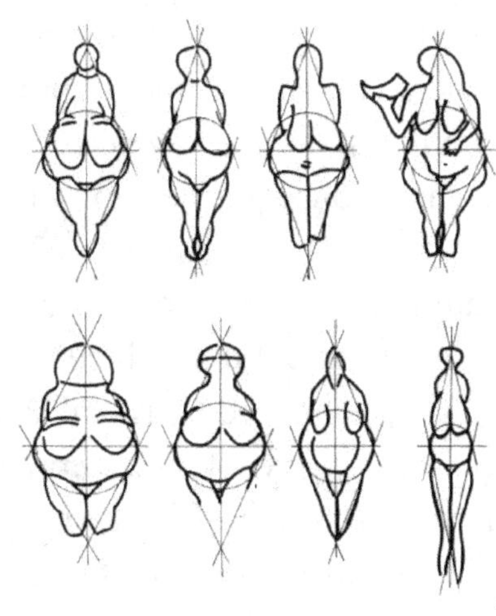

It is hard to understand the true extent of the idea that none of us would exist but for social constructs. That "individuality", attached to our self-awareness, is just a manifestation of our "social being". We don't exist without the group, and in spite of our precious self-esteem, like many other species, human life depends not only on individual abilities, but also on the reproduction and continuous improvement of what is called "collective intelligence". This intelligence is based on the selection of behaviours that allow existence in a certain environment, and that generally determine the place and function of each of us.

Despite its complexity, the exclusive goal of our "collective intelligence" is reproduction. This goal is indifferent to individual wishes and overrides other alternatives, precisely because of its effectiveness in making us multiply.

We share with other species, as manifestations of "collective intelligence", altruistic behaviours that ensure the protection of the weaker members of the species. It is outside the scope of this article to discuss the extent to which these behaviours are the expression of learning ("cultural behaviours" as we say in relation to the human species) or the consequence of the translation of information carried by the genes. What appears to be exclusive to humans, as a consequence of being a species adapted to the environment through culture, is that each one of those behaviours is backed by moral sanctions.

In other words, any of our altruistic behaviours — always understood in terms of expressing the reproductive goal — and regardless of the society in which they occur, are always associated with a "cultural explanation" tailored to the needs and background of that particular culture. Whatever we do that is "good" or "bad", as accepted and expected, or unacceptable and unexpected, exists only in terms of that particular culture.

It would be reasonable to think that if we speak of "male domination", we do so believing that males are the ones that have determined what is "good" and what is "bad" and that these assumptions were made to benefit males.

Let's confront this statement with the facts. For this, I propose that we look back to the beginning of human development, picturing the following scene: At the entrance of a cave a few families are encamped. The people, dry and warm, rest around the fires that burn bright. The grownups talk in hush voices, the hum sometimes broken by the children at play. Suddenly a deafening roar is heard from the back of the cave. For an instant, the silence is complete, soon broken by the cries of the women: "A bear! A bear!", as they desperately try to flee, dragging with them children and old people towards the nearby bushes. There, after the initial panic abates, a mother is heard comforting her children in a still trembling voice because of the flight: "Do not worry, father can deal with any bear".

We are entitled to ask; why would a young male, wielding just a fire-hardened pole, face a gigantic cave bear (Ursus spelaeus), when he can run faster than anyone in his group, and knows that the bear will abandon his chase to enjoy some delicious human offspring.

The answer can only reside in the importance of socially expected behaviour. We must remember that our young man is not on his own, he's surrounded by his fellows, and that his performance, good or bad, will later be public, amplified by the surviving women.

It wouldn't make sense that in a male-dominated world, this socially expected behaviour would have been raised by the men themselves. Why wouldn't they promote expectations that are more favourable to the nature of males?

For example, he who runs fast enough to escape his predators would be rewarded by society. This is undoubtedly so because it was women — not men — who create expectations to ensure that males' actions will be altruistic for the sake of reproduction. These expectations could even be contrary to the males' wellbeing, and even to their very survival.

Thus, if my picture is correct, how then was it possible that women, being weaker than men, could impose upon them such conditioning? Precisely, by not being weak. Instead, they profited from the only aspect in which they are biologically stronger than men: that of sexual intercourse.

This was basically achieved by exerting their control, with the help of the biological differences between women and men, over the inescapable sexual urges of men, which depend on their genetically controlled hormonal flow.

The fact is that female sexuality is concealed, while male sexuality is explicit. And this applies not only because men are unable to hide their sexual arousal, but also because the orgasm —as the manifestation of the highest attainable pleasure — is directly associated with ejaculation. Thus the woman can monitor not only the state of the male's arousal, but also how much pleasure he attained with her. The male is ignorant about either state (or at best can attempt a guess). Consequently, by displaying their desire and their fulfilment men find themselves in a position of weakness in the face of their female adversary, who — as any poker player would confirm — may or may not be aroused, and might or might not have reached an orgasm.

The key to women's superiority lies in the location of the clitoris, the organ of feminine sexual sensitivity. Unlike primitive mammals, the clitoris sits outside the vagina; this location gives women, as opposed to men, the ability to separate sexual pleasure from the reproductive usage of their genitalia.

Evolutionary biologists have never reached a clear conclusion regarding the adaptive value of this particular location, which makes sense, for humans, in the light of the approach described here.

The ability to isolate sexual pleasure from intercourse allows women not only to exert control over sexual intercourse, but to develop many other sensual nuances and possibilities regarding sexual relations. These nuances and possibilities are denied to individuals for whom sex is limited to a single goal: ejaculation.

Such control, explains not only the historical consequences we have been discussing but also the capacity to engage in activities such as prostitution. This is enabled in women because, as we have been discussing, the sexual pleasure of men is directly dependent on the reproductive function of ejaculation.

In order to understand the relevance of this superiority, we must remember that the evolutionary principle states that random changes (i.e. genetic mutations) enable new possible interactions with the environment. When such interactions receive a positive or a neutral feedback, then the mutation becomes permanent; but when the feedback is negative, the mutation disappears together with those who carry it.

The human species is a culturally adapted species, and to a great extent its environment is itself a product of human culture. In this state of affairs, biological alterations like the articulated language faculty or the one we are dealing with here — the capacity to keep sexual pleasure separate from reproduction — might contribute to a positive feedback loop, depending on the specific features created by the cultural framework itself.

The ability of women to manage their sexual activity is superior over that of men, in a context where sex is an imperative for the latter. This results in women being able to cultivate and impose an increasingly altruistic behaviour in men.

This is clearly the result of a natural process, nobody is to blame for this outcome, and should by no means be understood as meaning that women have a innate bias to perversely dominate men.

This occurred because in the new increasingly cultural environment developed by humans, some females succeeded in using sex for their own benefit, thereby making men care for and about them more. As a consequence, females who managed to receive better care also bore more progeny than those who didn't receive the same degree of care (because they either didn't make the effort or lacked competence). Their more numerous progeny favoured the multiplication of a kind of human increasingly dependent on an ever more complex social organisation.

We have to understand that we are looking at a very slow process, with outcomes that accumulate over the very long-term, running for hundreds of thousands of years.

The adaptive success of the emerging human species — and that of its cousins, the great apes — depended on the effectiveness of their social relations. Any improvement in the adaptive capacity of these species must be assessed in terms of reproductive performance, and this improvement is always associated with an increasing complexity in their social structure. This latter concept is what makes humans unique and different from the great apes.

Under such circumstances, the capacity to make men behave in a more altruistic way towards women and children clearly signifies an adaptive advantage. Advantage that grew out of trial and error over the long-term of human evolution.

Undoubtedly, it could be argued that my model is unacceptable because men are physically more powerful than women, so they always had the ability to force them to have sex against their will. But the case is that given the organic correlation between male orgasm and sexual activity (men cannot have sex without experiencing pleasure at the same time), rape appears as a poor adaptive strategy compared to the pleasure that can be achieved through consensuality and frequency, both of which are factors under the control of women. Once again, over the long course of the evolution of our species, this imbalance would have reduced rape to the exception.

Against this backdrop we can understand some aspects of current sexual behaviour in women as traces of past strategies developed by them to avoid being raped. One of them is the readiness to accept a sexual approach from a stranger — always justified as occurring under "exceptional and particular circumstances"— followed by the frequent rejection of ulterior approaches by the same male, unless he agrees to her conditions in aspects of reproduction.

It is easy to imagine that, in the early stages of evolution of our species, the mere act of rejecting an ardent and powerful male would inevitably conclude in rape. On the other hand, agreeing to his demands allows a sensual/emotional bond to be established. The male will compare the satisfaction attained in a consensual relation to that experienced in a rape, and the new bond will reduce the likelihood of rape in an eventual second encounter.

Using these mechanisms among others of a similar nature, women achieved a position that allowed them to set the fundamental terms of the sexual agreement, namely: "Mister man, you are allowed to have frequent consensual sexual intercourse with me, provided that you care for me and my children".

Viewed from another perspective, the consensual practice of sex is established as a reward for males' altruistic behaviour. But not only did they lay the foundations of the sexual agreement, women also imposed the moral sanctions that support it, namely altruism, in such a way that men are not only unaware of their surrender but even proud of it.

To summarize, a comparison between generic men and women shows that men are stronger than women, have stronger bones and muscles; something that has many consequences. However, women are stronger than men in terms of reproductive capacity, not only because they are able to control sexual activity, as we said before, but also — and primarily — because women bear the burden of the procreation.

Men live under the organic/hormonal imperative of having sex with women, the survival of the species depends on sex, and women are stronger than men in the sexual arena: hence men are, in general terms, weaker than women. Women have used and still use their preponderance as a means for laying out the foundations of social organization. However, there is still another factor that makes such a development inevitable.

In the evolutionary process, the human species has developed by way of specializing as a "cultural" species due to our superior ability to convey information. Such preeminence is due to the articulated language faculty, which allows us to share among ourselves the elements necessary for the reproduction of our cultural modes of adaptation.

With its almost infinite multiplicity (anything can be said), articulated language also addresses the communication problems posed by the needs of social organizations that are increasingly complex and more numerous. For instance, those that are required to sustain the increasing participation of male altruistic behavior over time.

And it so happens, as you have already anticipated, that in this field women are also stronger than men; to the point that the very organic structure of their brains is better adapted to that function than that of men.

These superior language abilities seem logical when we consider that during human social development, the need to look after children and newborns necessarily led women to be more sedentary and gregarious than men.

Among existing hunter-gatherer groups, the "home" — i.e. the most permanent human gathering — is still essentially a group of women, children and the elderly, while men usually scatter in their long hunting expeditions. Under such conditions of communal living, the power of speech becomes a basic need. And it is precisely during these long, predominantly female conversations that the so called "male values" like "bravery", "responsibility", "competition", " sacrifice", etc. will first become vocalised.

From that moment on, a dialectical relationship will be established between the male altruistic behavior, which as we saw is imposed by women, and the "masculine moral values", also developed by women to support the survival of altruism.

This is how it must have started, some seventy thousand years ago, with the emergence of "Sapiens Sapiens", the first beings to possess the complex faculty of articulate language. This continuously developing relationship that continues to this day, had an extraordinary outcome whereby female desires appear disguised in the form of "macho" attitudes.

To achieve this transmutation, the basic principle is to disguise feminine desires as masculine ones, which entails presenting them as attractive or beneficial to men.

In turn, the achievement of these "masculine" objectives is socially rewarded, in particular by women, with permanent recognition for the "bravest", the "strongest", the "fastest", the "richest", and so on. Given the natural competition existing amongst males for access to sexual partners, such recognition reinforces the feedback for those "male" behaviors that ensure the protection of women and their offspring.

This is the origin of the fictional supposed "male domination" when, in fact, "patriarchal" behavior is nothing more than a direct consequence of female intervention; permanently and throughout the evolution of the species and in favor of their own objectives. Objectives that are the ever-increasing altruistic behavior of the males and consequently, the increased protection of women and their offspring. The expression of this process, which differentiates us from other species due to permanent increases in social complexity, was made possible by the pre-eminence of the "cultural" option, as a means of adaptation to the environment.

It is thus not surprising that movements for "women's rights" are based upon the denunciation of "macho" values, values which were promoted by women themselves. Even less surprisingly, men, always manipulated by women, accept this notion as if it were true.

In other words, the supposed privileges that men enjoy, are nothing more than a very modest compensation for their "naturally" abnormal behaviour of maintaining a permanent altruistic demeanour.

For a better understanding, let me compare the domestication of wolves into dogs. Humans managed to tame the wolf —a predator — by selecting the least aggressive among them, thereby imprinting in them a subjection to man during the initial stages of their existence and compensating the repression of their aggressive instincts through the provision of food. However, a dog, in its deep interior, remains essentially a wolf and, in exceptional circumstances, again shows its intrinsically aggressive character.

For the same reason, men, no matter how deeply their natural behavior has been modified by culture, develop occasional aggressive behaviors towards women, typical of their natural tendencies and normally repressed by the social context.

What compensation do men receive for this subjugation besides the sexual activity mentioned above?

First of all, as I have already pointed out, the moral compensation of believing themselves "superior" to women and that society operates on "patriarchal' foundations.

Secondly, now in practical terms, the compensation of being included within the system of domestic care instituted by women, provided that they have fulfilled their "masculine" obligations.

Thirdly, some degree of tolerance for deviation from certain altruistic behaviors expressed in the form of spontaneously masculine activities, like fraternization with other males, violent games and competitions, or sexual promiscuity; as long as such deviations do not affect the general functioning of the system.

Of course, women include in the list of benefits all the domestic responsibilities they assume in the care of their children, like decisions on food and clothing and even enquiring if the electricity bill has been paid. All of these are in reality the expression of their own natural tendencies, the materialization of their own reproductive desire.

Let's look as some examples of such supposed male imposition.

To begin with, the standards set for feminine beauty. These are normally considered masculine constructs and are based on the perception of women as "sexual objects", to the detriment of "true" feminine values, such as intelligence, kindness, etc.

The fact is that fertile women must compete for men in order to reproduce and, over the long evolution of the species, evolutionary advantage was assigned to those men who were attracted by the feminine physical attributes related to their possible reproductive performance, such as hips and breasts. Because those males had a greater number of descendants than those who were attracted by other aspects, that might be transcendent, albeit without consequences for the number of descendants.

The preference of males for those physical attributes has always been known by women and will be the basis for the inevitable competition that they must sustain among them in order to acquire the most convenient sexual partners for their reproductive purposes.

Perfecting this practice for hundreds of thousands of years has brought us to a point where current technical developments allow women to permanently experiment with new ways of presenting themselves physically. Developments that include ever more sophisticated makeup, jewelry, clothing, etc, and which have the makings of the main activity of the female gender.

As usual, men have had little to do with the development of this paraphernalia, and women, who denounce lack of consideration, are the ones that expect reactions, not opinions, from men in order to enliven the system.

What women also decry, most surprisingly, is the apparent monopoly that men make of leadership positions.

These apparently objectionable traits of the male have been selected for hundreds of thousands of years as the foundation for ensuring the survival of the human species.

As women, with their swollen bellies and caring for their little children had to work on domestic chores, men had to concentrate on strategic issues relating to settlement location, resources and defense.

When threatened by an attack from predators, human or animal, women had to take charge of the children, while men had to direct the manoeuvring of the group. Groupings that acted in this way had a higher chance of survival, thanks to the knowledge that men had of the terrain, whereas those led by women were more vulnerable.

Therefore, in circumstances such as these, what is the male pattern of behaviours preferred by females, all throughout history?

Timing is central to the proper understanding of male and female behaviour. The difference becomes challenging if we try to apply the timing of these behaviours with a perspective of current events.

Of course, we are no longer those bands of hunter-gatherers peppered throughout a world that is almost un-peopled as well as densely populated by predators threatening our own lives. At the same time, we should not forget that our dominance over that world is at most ten thousand years old, or around 0,002% of the history of humankind.

It was during the previous 99.998% of our history that, as a consequence of the selection imposed by adaptive practices, the basis for the relationship between men and women was established. To state the argument in contemporary terms, it was during that long period that women have been shaping male behaviour to suit their needs.

Men should open their eyes to their own history. Why have they strived so arduously to be the strongest, the fastest, the richest, the smartest or the most agreeable? It was simply to conquer the heart of their beloved, and always with the implicit or explicit objective of engaging in sexual relations with them.

Who taught men that valour, skill, perseverance, leadership and competitiveness were masculine attributes? Who else, but their mothers?

The "matriarchal" story, which was built in the intimacy of the mother-child relationship under uncontrolled circumstances and thus able to express fully the sentiment of the mother, is exactly the same as the one they will hear, later on, when they turn three or four, coming out of their fathers' mouths.

Men seem incapable of interpreting correctly this fact because, until that time, they have been nurtured by the only ideology available — the matriarchal one.

Let me state it again: the story of patriarchy has resulted in the evolutionary reinforcement of the role of men as carers for their women and their offspring. The spread of competitive standards by which males judge themselves elicits as its primary consequence the development of the traits that make it possible for them to provide better and better nourishment and protection for their children.

It was women — who do know what they want — who introduced those negative moral judgements into the structure of social dynamics; the same dynamics denounced as "patriarchal ideology".

This is why males who are not hard-workers are severely judged, as are cowards and those who abandon their children, etc. Inversely, men who work hard, who are courageous or who win in any competitive activity, are universally recognised.

But then, if the 'patriarchal ideology' is a female product, why are feminist claims so strident and vocal that they appear to overwhelm our daily lives? Why accuse men of doing exactly what women have been imprinting on them all along the lengthy path of human development?

The answer fits in with the ancestral training that women have had in manipulating and shaping male behaviour through moral sanctions to serve their aspirations. These aspirations have changed in tune with the extraordinary technological advances that characterise our age.

For all of human history women have needed strong, competitive men, with leadership qualities, and who used those capacities in an altruistic way to favour themselves and their offspring. This behaviour was a direct result of women proposing and reproducing the use of moral sanctions.

Times have changed. Technological developments that have allowed humans to achieve the very highest levels of productivity in almost every field have created a totally new situation in which prosperity seems increasingly the result of collective action and not the consequence of individual actions.

If then our existence seems supported by a society that would have no limits in its capacity to satisfy all kinds of demands, each one of us, as isolated individuals, can demand that it respond to our particular needs and, concomitantly, to support these demands with new moral sanctions that quickly transform a potential situation into a "right".

In this context, any individual woman may assume that she no longer has the need for a traditional association with an altruistic man to insure her reproductive objectives. It is the "collective" that rises up to the task of caring that her and her offspring will need.

Furthermore, as the extraordinary success of our species is notoriously resulting in the overpopulation of the planet, the very reproductive objectives of women become increasingly undesirable. Feminism starts to resemble a necessary adaptive cultural response to this, and it carries in its wake increasing tolerance towards most forms of homosexual behaviour and other ways to balance the equation between population and resources.

Being the main enactors of moral sanctions, the feminists' claims only result in the reinforcement of that process. These re-vindications initially take the form of political demands, and then, rapidly become a quest to establish the opposition between "women's" rights vs "men's" rights (I use quotation marks, since us men seemingly have a monopoly over all rights).

We must not forget that "men's rights" (the patriarchal ideology) have only been limited to the right to continue behaving altruistically for the benefit of women. Neither can we forget that almost all moral sanctions emerged in the women-controlled household realm, and that those sanctions were imposed on men as a way of securing women's reproductive goals, keeping men strong and competitive, artfully making them look as proposed by men.

Dear fellow victims of this historical falsehood. Men have never really been able to control anything at all in the social sphere. Much less the intricate combination of ideological and emotional factors upon which our "satisfaction" as citizens depends.

Our future as sex (gender) is uncertain. We could view it with optimism provided men become able to challenge women's monopoly of the establishment of moral sanctions.

If this is not achieved, the altruistic behavior which has been forced upon us up to now, is a direct path towards slavery, forcing men, under the form of legal dictates, to perform almost all the reproductive tasks that women perform today.

On the other hand, the combination of constant increases in productivity and the gradual taking-up by women of traditionally male jobs, can lay the foundations for us to also claim our "rights", such as owning our time and rejecting obligations that are not strictly necessary for the perpetuation of the species.

Regrettably, people must keep up their vigilance: in these circumstances, the process of female empowerment has no adaptive limits in itself.

The mythical Amazons — a tribe of armed women who use men for exclusively for conceiving young only to kill them afterwards — are there to remind us that women have always dreamed of absolute female domination and the fear of men that it may become reality.

The "men's rights" (for even the term "rights of man" has been hijacked), so abused throughout history, are now in danger of disappearing completely. That is why it is absolutely necessary that all people prepare themselves to fight in their defense and development.

It will not be a fair fight, as I have stated, not only do men not have secrets for our adversary, but what is worse, it prevails in orality, the field in which most battles will take place.

Perhaps this is our last great battle before accepting the very "natural" —and tragic— fate of the unarmed drone, killed by the powerful bee once he has fulfilled his reproductive function.